I Am Responsible

Katie Peters

GRL Consultants,
Diane Craig and Monica Marx,
Certified Literacy Specialists

Lerner Publications ◆ Minneapolis

Note from a GRL Consultant
This Pull Ahead leveled book has been carefully designed for beginning readers. A team of guided reading literacy experts has reviewed and leveled the book to ensure readers pull ahead and experience success.

Lerner Publications Company
An imprint of Lerner Publishing Group, Inc.
241 First Avenue North
Minneapolis, MN 55401 USA

For reading levels and more information, look up this title at www.lernerbooks.com.

Main body text set in Memphis Pro 24/39
Typeface provided by Linotype.

Photo Acknowledgments
The images in this book are used with the permission of: © HappyKids/Getty Images, pp. 4–5, 16 (cleaning cloth); © 3sbworld/Getty Images, p. 3; © Fertnig/Getty Images, pp. 10–11, 16 (dog bowl); © Image Source/Getty Images, pp. 12–13; © karens4/Getty Images, pp. 8–9, 16 (chess pieces); © kilukilu/Getty Images, pp. 6–7; © parinyabinsuk/Getty Images, pp. 14–15.

Front cover: © FamVeld/Getty Images

Library of Congress Cataloging-in-Publication Data

Names: Peters, Katie, author.
Title: I am responsible / Katie Peters.
Description: Minneapolis : Lerner Publications, 2022. | Series: Character builders (pull ahead readers people smarts - nonfiction) | Includes index. | Audience: Ages 4–7 | Audience: Grades K–1 | Summary: "Model responsible behavior to early readers by showing them how to act in agreement with their words to help with chores and to be a good friend. Pairs with the fiction title Time to Clean"— Provided by publisher.
Identifiers: LCCN 2020015324 (print) | LCCN 2020015325 (ebook) | ISBN 9781728403533 (library binding) | ISBN 9781728423333 (paperback) | ISBN 9781728417837 (ebook)
Subjects: LCSH: Responsibility—Juvenile literature.
Classification: LCC BJ1451 .P478 2021 (print) | LCC BJ1451 (ebook) | DDC 179/.9—dc23

LC record available at https://lccn.loc.gov/2020015324
LC ebook record available at https://lccn.loc.gov/2020015325

Manufactured in the United States of America
2-1009213-48891-2/1/2023

Table of Contents

I Am Responsible

I said I would clean.

I wipe the table.

I said I would pick up my toys. I put them in the basket.

I said I would play with my sister. We play a game.

I said I would feed
the dog. I fill his bowl.

I said I would meet my friend. We play at the park.

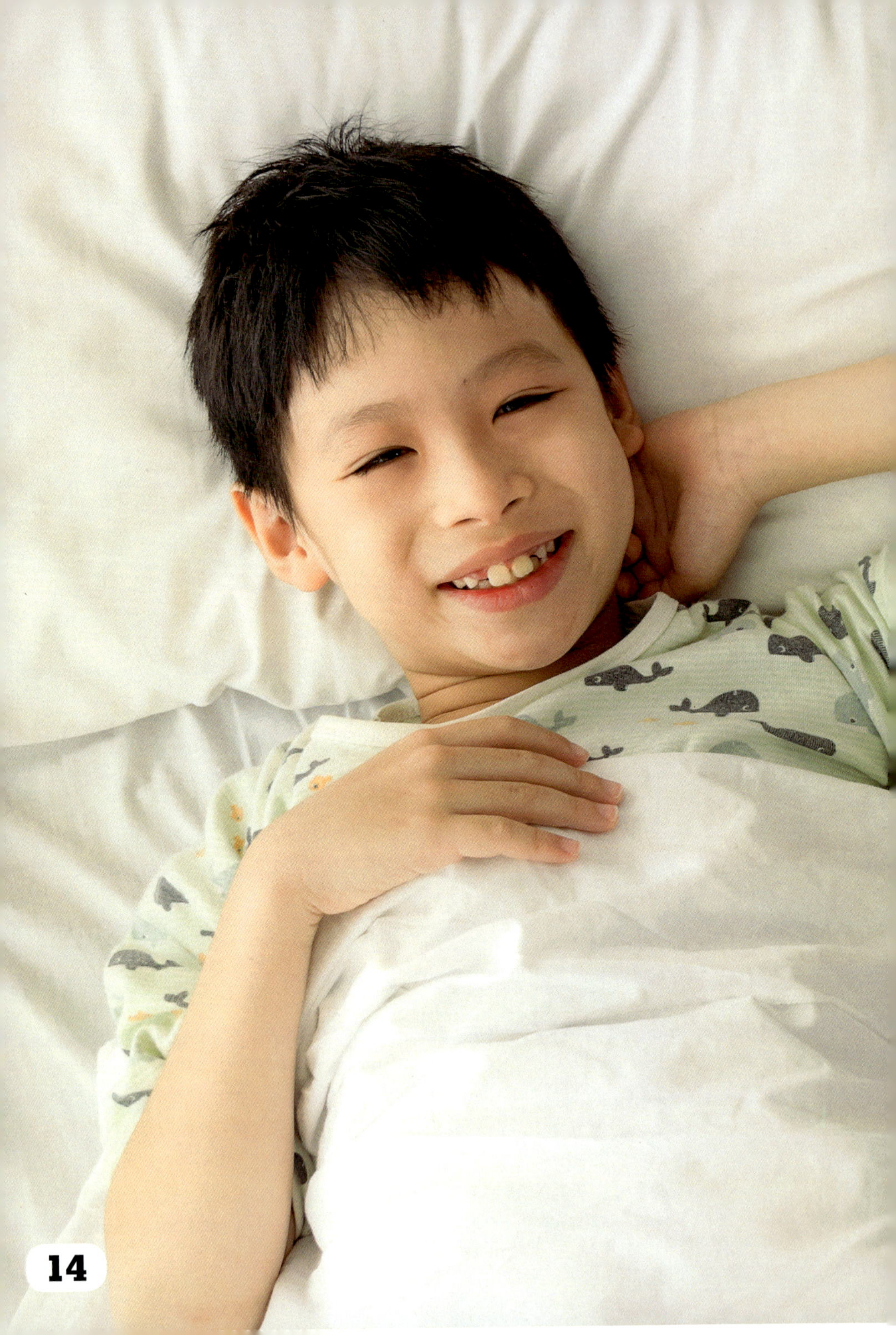

I said I would go to bed.
Good night!

What are you responsible for at home or at school?

Did You See It?

chess pieces

cleaning cloth

dog bowl

Index